ARCADE

The Missions: California's Heritage

MISSION
SAN RAFAEL ARCÁNGEL

by

Mary Null Boulé

Book Twenty in a series of twenty-one

DEAR READER,

You will find an outline of this chapter's important topics at the back of the booklet. It is there for you to use in writing a report or giving an oral report on this mission.

If you first read the booklet completely, then you can use the outline as a guide to write your report in your own words, instead of copying sentences from the chapter.

Good luck, read carefully,
and use your own words.
MNB

The Missions: California's Heritage

MISSION
SAN RAFAEL ARCÁNGEL

by

Mary Null Boulé

Merryant Publishing
Vashon, Washington

Book Twenty in a series of twenty-one

With special thanks to Msgr. Francis J. Weber, Archivist of the Los Angeles Catholic Diocese for his encouragement and expertise in developing this series.

This series is dedicated to my sister, Nancy Null Kenyon, whose editing skills and support were so freely given.

ISBN: 1-877599-19-0

Father Junípero Serra

INTRODUCTION

Building of a mission church involved everyone in the mission community. Priests were engineers and architects; Native Americans did the construction. Mission Indian in front is pouring adobe mix into a brick form. Bricks were then dried in the sun.

FATHER SERRA AND THE MISSIONS: AN INTRODUCTION

The year was 1769. On the east coast of what would soon become the United States, the thirteen original colonies were making ready to break away from England. On the west coast of our continent, however, there could be found only untamed land inhabited by Native Americans, or Indians. Although European explorers had sailed up and down the coast in their ships, no one but American Indians had explored the length of this land on foot . . . until now.

To this wild, beautiful country came a group of adventurous men from New Spain, as Mexico was then called. They were following the orders of their king, King Charles III of Spain.

One of the men was a Spanish missionary named Fray Junípero Serra. He had been given a tremendous job; especially since he was fifty-six years old, an old man in those days. King Charles III had ordered mission settlements to be built along the coast of Alta (Upper) California and it was Fr. Serra's task to carry out the king's wishes.

Father Serra had been born in the tiny village of Petra

on the island of Mallorca, Spain. He had done such an excellent job of teaching and working with the Indians in Mexican missions, the governor of New Spain had suggested to the king that Fr. Serra do the same with the Indians of Alta California. Hard-working Fray Serra was helped by Don Gaspár de Portolá, newly chosen governor of Alta California, and two other Franciscan priests who had grown up with Fr. Serra in Mallorca, Father Fermin Lasuén and Father Francisco Palóu.

There were several reasons why men had been told to build settlements along the coast of this unexplored country. First, missions would help keep the land as Spanish territory. Spain wanted to be sure the rest of the world knew it owned this rich land. Second, missions were to be built near harbors so towns would grow there. Ships from other countries could then stop to trade with the Spaniards, but these travelers could not try to claim the land for themselves. Third, missions were a good way to turn Indians into Christian, hard-working people.

It would be nice if we could write here that everything went well; that twenty-one missions immediately sprang up along the coast. Unfortunately, all did not go well. It would take fifty-four years to build all the California missions. During those fifty-four years many people died from Indian attacks, sickness, and starvation. Earthquakes and fires constantly ruined mission buildings, which then had to be built all over again. Fr. Serra calmly overcame each problem as it happened, as did those priests who followed him.

When a weary Fray Serra finally died in 1784, he had founded nine missions from San Diego to Monterey and had arranged the building of many more. Fr. Lasuén continued Fr. Serra's work, adding eight more missions to the California mission chain. The remaining four missions were founded in later years.

Originally, plans had been to place missions a hard day's walk from each other. Many of them were really quite far apart. Travelers truly struggled to go from one mission to another along the 650 miles of walking road known as El Camino Real, The Royal Highway. Today keen eyes will sometimes see tall, curved poles with bells hanging from them sitting by the side of streets and highways. These bell poles are marking a part of the old El Camino Real.

At first Spanish soldiers were put in charge of the towns which grew up near each mission. The priests were told to handle only the mission and its properties. It did not take long to realize the soldiers were not kind and gentle leaders. Many were uneducated and did not have the understanding they should have had in dealing with people. So the padres came to be in charge of not only the mission, but of the townspeople and even of the soldiers.

The first missions at San Diego and Monterey were built near the ocean where ships could bring them needed supplies. After early missions began to grow their own food and care for themselves, later mission compounds were built farther away from the coast. What one mission did well, such as leatherworking, candlemaking, or raising cattle, was shared with other missions. As a result, missions became somewhat specialized in certain products.

Although mission buildings looked different from mission to mission, most were built from one basic plan. Usually a compound was constructed as a large, four-sided building with an inner patio in the center. The outside of the quadrangle had only one or two doors, which were locked at night to protect the mission. A church usually sat at one corner of the quadrangle and was always the tallest and largest part of the mission compound.

Facing the inner patio were rooms for the two priests living there, workshops, a kitchen, storage rooms for grain and food, and the mission office. Rooms along the back of the quadrangle often served as home to the unmarried Indian women who worked in the kitchen. The rest of the Indians lived just outside the walls of the mission in their own village.

Beyond the mission wall and next to the church was a cemetery. Today you can still see many of the original headstones of those who died while living and working at the mission. Also outside the walls were larger workshops, a reservoir holding water used at the mission, and orchards containing fruit trees. Huge fields surrounded each mission where crops grew and livestock such as sheep, cattle, and horses grazed.

It took a great deal of time for some Indian tribes to understand the new way of life a mission offered, even though the

Native Americans always had food and shelter when they became mission Indians. Each morning all Indians were awakened at sunrise by a church bell calling them to church. Breakfast followed church . . . and then work. The women spun thread and made clothes, as well as cooked meals. Men and older boys worked in workshops or fields and constructed buildings. Meanwhile the Indian children went to school, where the padres taught them. After a noon meal there was a two hour rest before work began again. After dinner the Indians sang, played, or danced. This way of life was an enormous change from the less organized Indian life before the missionaries arrived. Many tribes accepted the change, some had more trouble getting used to a regular schedule, some tribes never became a part of mission life.

Water was all-important to the missions. It was needed to irrigate crops and to provide for the mission people and animals. Priests designed and engineered magnificent irrigation systems at most of the missions. All building of aqueducts and reservoirs of these systems was done by the mission Indians.

With all the organized hard work, the missions did very well. They grew and became strong. Excellent vineyards gave wine for the priests to use and to sell. Mission fields produced large grain crops of wheat and corn, and vast grazing land developed huge herds of cattle and sheep. Mission life was successful for over fifty years.

When Mexico broke away from Spain, it found it did not have enough money to support the California missions, as Spain had been doing. So in 1834, Mexico enforced the secularization law which their government had decreed several years earlier. This law stated missions were to be taken away from the missionaries and given to the Indians. The law said that if an Indian did not want the land or buildings, the property was to be sold to anyone who wished to buy it.

It is true the missions had become quite large and powerful. And as shocked as the padres were to learn of the secularization law, they also knew the missions had originally been planned as temporary, or short term projects. The priests had been sure their Indians would be well-trained enough to run the missions by themselves when the time came to move to other unsettled lands. In fact, however, even after fifty years the California Indians were still not ready to handle the huge missions.

Since the Indians did not wish to continue the missions, the buildings and land were sold, the Indians not even waiting for money or, in some cases, receiving money for the sale.

Sad times lay ahead. Many Indians went back to the old way of life. Some Indians stayed on as servants to the new owners and often these owners were not good to them. Mission buildings were used for everything from stores and saloons to animal barns. In one mission the church became a barracks for the army. A balcony was built for soldiers with their horses stabled in the altar area. Rats ate the stored grain and beautiful church robes. Furniture and objects left by the padres were stolen. People even stole the mission building roof tiles, which then caused the adobe brick walls to melt from rain. Earthquakes finished off many buildings.

Shortly after California became a part of the United States in the mid-1850s, our government returned all mission buildings to the Catholic Church. By this time most of them were in terrible condition. Since the priests needed only the church itself and a few rooms to live in, the other rooms of the mission were rented to anyone who needed them. Strange uses were found in some cases. In the San Fernando Mission, for example, there was once a pig farm in the patio area.

Tourists finally began to notice the mission ruins in the early 1900s. Groups of interested people got together to see if the missions could be restored. Some missions had been "modernized" by this time, unfortunately, but within the last thirty years historians have found enough pictures, drawings, and written descriptions to rebuild or restore most of the missions to their original appearances.

The restoration of all twenty-one missions is a splendid way to preserve our California heritage. It is the hope of many Californians that this dream of restoration can become a reality in the near future.

Interior of replica chapel is modern, since no drawings of original chapel were ever found. Chapel is well-cared for and open to public.

MISSION SAN RAFAEL ARCÁNGEL

I. THE MISSION TODAY

Mission San Rafael Chapel is a charming replica of the mission chapel built long ago. The replica was built in 1949. At that time, in order to save money, the walls were made of hollow concrete, but after the concrete was plastered it looked just like the original adobe brick. The words "replica" and "looked just like" might make you think Mission San Rafael is nothing but a distant memory. Actually the chapel is a fine memorial to the one mission which simply disappeared from the earth in the late 1800s. People at the mission site today are most eager to share their knowledge of mission days and are always on the lookout for artifacts that will increase the heritage of San Rafael Mission.

It was hard to build the chapel, since so few pictures or drawings could be found. Even though the direction the chapel faces is different than the original, it is thought to be the same size as the 1817 building. The facade is quite plain. On either side of the arched doorway are concrete pilasters, or fake pillars, topped with a concrete beam. Over the doorway are two windows, one above the other, shaped like the star window of the Carmel Mission.

Three of the remaining four bells hang from a wood frame to the left of the chapel door. These small bells were rediscovered in strange places. One was found in a Catholic church in El Cajon, near San Diego. Another bell had been used for many years as a school bell in the town of Fallon. The third bell had been a dinner bell on a large ranch. The fourth bell rests on a spot at the side of the chapel facing a busy street in the center of downtown San Rafael. These four bells are almost the only original objects left of old Mission San Rafael.

The inside of the chapel has a festive look. Hanging from poles on either side wall are six colorful flags representing the governments under which the mission has been ruled. Also on the walls are beautiful, modern hand-carved Stations of the Cross, given to the chapel in 1949. Hanging from the slightly vaulted wood and beam ceiling are wrought iron chandeliers designed to look like the old mission candle holders.

On each side of the partly gilded reredos are hand-carved oak wood statues. In the top niche of the reredos is a wooden statue of the patron saint of the mission, Saint Raphael. The pulpit at the right front of the sanctuary is also decorated with a carved figure of St. Raphael. In front of the pulpit is a delicate wrought iron railing. Several tall windows along one side of the chapel allow the interior a warm, sunny glow.

Attached to the chapel is a wing containing a large gift shop. What few objects are left from the original mission are placed in the small museum at one end of the gift shop. Included in the museum are some fine paintings of Mission San Rafael. One particularly colorful painting is over seventy-five years old. It shows Father Amoros, long-time padre at the mission, baptizing Indian Chief Marin in front of the mission building. One sketch on the wall is thought to be the most accurate ever done of old Mission San Rafael. Eight other sketches of the mission are contained in the tiny museum. It is said that all of these sketches were used to help design the present chapel. Many objects from other California missions are to be found here.

One might wonder what purpose a small chapel has on one of the main streets of a thriving town. How could this be a fitting memorial to a 170 year old mission, especially when hardly a trace of the original remains? A short time spent in the lovely sacred chapel, which is left open during the day for all to use, explains it all. The chapel was seldom empty the day it was visited by the author. Thick walls keep traffic noises away and make it a place to renew one's spirit. San Rafael, which began as a place of healing, carries on the same tradition which was begun by the founding padres, a healing of the spirit.

II.   HISTORY OF THE MISSION

San Rafael never started out to be a mission. It was built as a hospital for Mission Dolores in San Francisco. The poor Indians of Mission Dolores were dying faster than at any other mission. Mission priests knew the Indians were being killed by the cold, damp, foggy climate of San Francisco, so they set out to find a sunnier place for their sick natives. The place they chose was an area known as Nanaguanui by the Indians. It was a lovely spot across the bay and north of Mission Dolores. Hills to the west of the site sheltered it from the cold.

On December 14, 1817, four priests, Fr. Narciso Duran of Mission San José, Fr. Abella of San Francisco de Asís (Dolores), and Father Gil y Taboada, along with Father-presidente of the California Missions, Fr. Sarria, all raised a cross and performed founding ceremonies for the new astencia. Astencia means being a part, or an extension, of something. San Rafael, Arcángel was chosen for the hospital's name because Saint Raphael was the patron saint of good health, and was said to heal body and soul. Father Gil was put in charge of the new hospital since he was known as the mission priest with the best knowledge of medicine. More than that, he spoke many Native American languages.

Even at the beginning, no effort was made to build anything but a small hospital building with a chapel at one end. The natives were taught how to make the adobe brick and roof tiles. In a short time a long, rather tall building 87 feet by 42 feet was completed. The building was taller than the usual mission cloister because the attic area of the roof above the chapel was to be used to store hay and grain. The chapel was at right angles to the hospital wing. There was no bell tower and the baptistry was only a lean-to against the end wall. In the hospital wing were storerooms and priests' quarters, as well as rooms for the sick Indians. There was a grass-covered corridor across the front of the hospital. A quadrangle was never planned at San Rafael. When the hospital became a mission in the 1820s, a quadrangle was still not built.

By 1819, Father Gil had cared for his ill Native Americans for two long, hard years. The Indians had rapidly gotten well, but the priest himself was not healthy. He was sent to another mission that year and was replaced by a remarkable priest, Father Juan Amoros. Fr. Amoros was not only a well-educated man, but an energetic, hard worker. He wanted no special treatment or attention. He was an inventor and once made a water clock that continued to keep good time for years after his death. Father Amoros loved children, always carrying bits of fruit in his sleeves as treats for them. Mission Indians and Spanish alike loved the padre.

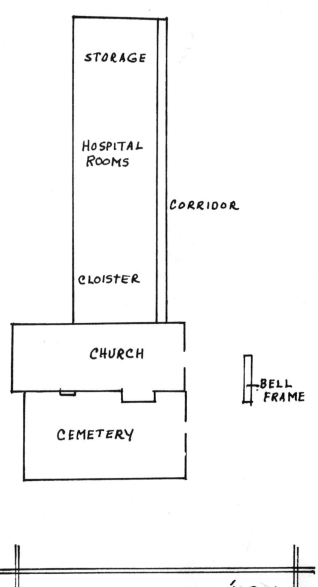

STORAGE

HOSPITAL
ROOMS

CORRIDOR

CLOISTER

CHURCH

BELL
FRAME

CEMETERY

SAN RAFAEL ARCÁNGEL
IN 1880's

Father Amoros developed excellent farm lands such as vineyards and orchards at his mission. The native men became farmers and cowboys, or learned such trades as sandalmaking, blacksmithing, harness making, carpentry, and boatbuilding. The building of boats was very important at San Rafael. Indians using padres' designs actually built ships that looked rather like Spanish vessels. Few, if any, other missions in California built ships.

The Indian women were taught to spin and weave wool and how to sew. Stronger women ground corn and wheat on stone mortar and pestles called metates. Flour made from the grain was used to feed people at the mission.

Because of the well-trained Indians at San Rafael, the hospital was able to care for all its needs. After ten years San Rafael became successful enough to be given the position of a full-fledged mission, instead of the astencia, or extension, of San Francisco's Mission Dolores. From October of 1872 on, all records were kept at Mission San Rafael rather than at Mission Dolores. Father Amoros had created a completely self-supported mission all by himself.

There were 1,140 mission Indians living at the mission in 1828. The Russians had begun to settle further inland from their own town of Fort Ross on the coast. It was well known that the Spaniards had approved the foundings of both Mission San Rafael and Mission San Francisco de Solano in Sonoma in order to have some way of keeping an eye on these Russians. San Rafael became a stop-over for military men traveling northward. Fr. Amoros always enjoyed the visitors at his mission, for he was the only priest there and life was often lonely for him.

Another reason Fr. Amoros liked to have visitors was his fear of Indian attacks. Many of those who stopped at San Rafael told of seeing guards on duty twenty-four hours a day, keeping a lookout for such attacks. One now-famous Indian trouble-maker was Chief Marin. The chief had once been baptized by Fr. Amoros, but he turned against the good padre and joined with another wild Indian named Quintin. Chief Marin, in spite of all the trouble he caused through the years, finally returned to Mission San Rafael and died there in 1834. A county in that area has been given the name Marin after the Indian chief. Quintin's name was given to the huge prison near San Rafael, although the prison is today known as San Quentin.

The big Indian attack Fr. Amoros had always feared finally happened in February, 1829. Fr. Amoros was rushed to a hiding place by mission Indians, who formed a wall of human beings around him to protect him. He was then hidden in some marshes and saved, but fighting went on between the trouble-making Indians and Spanish soldiers for some time.

Father Amoros returned to a badly damaged mission, and repaired the buildings. The mission continued to grow until the tired old padre became very ill and died. He had been in charge of Mission San Rafael for thirteen years by this time. History shows him as responsible for all the success the small mission would ever have. The good Padre Amoros was buried in the chapel in 1832, and was sadly missed by his mission Indians.

The year of Fr. Amoros's death was the year the mission had its largest number of animals: 5,508. The wheat crop that year was 17,905 bushels, and the bean crop was 1,360 bushels.

It was about this time that Mexico was breaking away from Spain. Mexico took over management of the California Missions, sending Mexican priests to replace the Spanish Franciscan monks. A Mexican priest, Fr. Jose Mercado, was the most unfortunate choice sent to take Fr. Amoros's place. He was unlike Fr. Amoros in every way. He was strict and unkind to the mission Indians. He also had great troubles with government officials and soldiers. Eventually he caused his own downfall by accusing an innocent group of visiting Indians of stealing. He gave guns to his mission Indians to keep, he said, the arrested Indians from coming back to San Rafael to get their revenge. His armed Indians were then accused of wrongly attacking some other visiting Indians at Fr. Mercado's command. Twenty-one people were killed in that attack and Fr. Mercado was sent to Mission Soledad as punishment. Later he was found innocent of causing the attack but Mission San Rafael had been terribly disturbed by their problem priest.

Secularization laws were put into effect in 1834 by Mexico. It was the beginning of the end for the California Missions. Land belonging to the missions, according to the law, was to be given back to the Indians. Value of San Rafael Mission was listed at $15,025. Nearly all of the money was in property because the church's value was placed at only $192.

General Mariano Vallejo had been in charge of all the military in Northern California for many years. He knew the missions and their property well. Secularization laws stated that priests were no longer in charge of the Indians. Without the priests' help and advice, the Indians did not realize land being given to them had to be farmed or they would lose it. General Vallejo understood this very well, however. He kept adding Indian land to his own property as the Indians left their land unused. There are many different opinions about General Vallejo today. Some feel he became rich by stealing Indian land. Others feel he was good to the Indians, using them as servants in his home so he could see they were well-fed and cared for. Maybe he felt he was only using the Indian land until they could farm it themselves. Whatever is true, the Indians never did get their land back.

In 1840 there were still 150 Indians left at Mission San Rafael. In 1844, San Rafael was left alone, abandoned. What was left of the empty buildings was sold for $8,000 in 1846. That sale was declared illegal a few months later when the United States took control of California.

For a while the American, John C. Fremont, used the mission building as his headquarters as he fought Mexicans in the battle to make California a United States territory. The mission was then without a priest for a few years. By 1847, a priest was once again living at Mission San Rafael. The United States returned six and a half acres of the mission land to the Catholic church in 1855, but by this time the building had crumbled to useless ruins. Church services were moved to the new St. Vincent Orphanage, about four miles from the mission site. The mission orchards and vineyards were used as a gypsy camping grounds during the 1860s.

A new parish church was later built near the old chapel ruins and in 1861 a carpenter, James Byers, bought all the wood he could find in the old mission building. In 1870, the last mounds of melted adobe bricks that had once been Mission San Rafael were removed to make room for the growing city of San Rafael.

In the seventeen short years of the mission many things had been accomplished. It had converted 1,873 Indians to the church; had raised at the most, 2,120 cattle in 1832; 4,000 sheep in 1822; and 454 horses in 1825. But the life of San Rafael Mission had been too short to compare it in size to the other California Missions.

All that finally remained of the hospital mission was a single pear tree from the old mission orchard, until the restoration of the chapel in 1949. Msgr. Thomas Kennedy, the present pastor of San Rafael Church, says he recently transplanted a small tendril from that ancient tree, hoping to keep some part of it as a living symbol of the spirit of Father Amoros and the old San Rafael Mission. Of course the tiny tree will live.

Three of four original bells hang from replica bell frame. A fourth bell, much larger, sits at one side of chapel building.

OUTLINE FOR MISSION SAN RAFAEL

I. The mission today

    A. Chapel replica, exterior
        1. When built
        2. Walls of hollow concrete, plastered
        3. Few pictures to use as model
        4. Facade description
        5. Chapel turned in different direction from original
        6. Bells
            a. Three on wood frame
            b. One bell at chapel side
        7. Mission site now in center of town
    B. Chapel interior
        1. Flags
        2. Stations of the Cross
        3. Chandeliers
        4. Reredos and statues
        5. Pulpit
        6. Railing
    C. Museum - gift shop
        1. Paintings
        2. Artifacts from other missions

II. History of the mission

    A. Founding as a hospital
        1. For Mission Dolores
        2. Four priests at founding
            a. December 14, 1817
        3. Patron saint, Rafael, was saint of good health
        4. Fr. Gil
    B. Original building description, size
        1. Indians help with adobe
        2. Chapel and hospital wings
            a. Storerooms and priests' quarters
        3. Corridor
        4. No quadrangle, ever
    C. Fr. Gil y Taboada leaves 1819

Outline continued next page

D. Fr. Amoros arrives and builds mission into a success
   1. Inventor
   2. Loved children
   3. Built farmlands
   4. Taught Indians
   5. Boatbuilding
E. 1828
   1. Watching Russians
   2. Visitors to mission
F. Chief Marin
   1. Troublemaker
G. Indians attack, 1829
   1. Fr. Amadoros saved by mission Indians
H. Mission badly damaged
   1. Buildings repaired
   2. Mission continues to grow
I. Fr. Amoros dies, 1834
   1. Also was missions's best year
J. Mexican rule of mission - secularization
   1. Fr. Mercado's problems
K. General Vallejo
L. 1840
   1. 150 Indians left
M. Mission abandoned in 1884
   1. Sold in 1846
N. John C. Fremont's headquarters
O. U.S. returns 6½ acres of mission land in 1885
P. Moves to St. Vincent Orphanage
Q. New parish church near site
   1. Wood of mission ruins sold
R. 1870, last of adobe removed
S. Seventeen years
   1. Successes
T. The pear tree

GLOSSARY

BUTTRESS: a large mass of stone or wood used to strengthen buildings

CAMPANARIO: a wall which holds bells

CLOISTER: an enclosed area; a word often used instead of convento

CONVENTO: mission building where priests lived

CORRIDOR: covered, outside hallway found at most missions

EL CAMINO REAL: highway between missions; also known as The King's Highway

FACADE: front wall of a building

FONT: large, often decorated bowl containing Holy Water for baptizing people

FOUNDATION: base of a building, part of which is below the ground

FRESCO: designs painted directly on walls or ceilings

LEGEND: a story coming from the past

PORTICO: porch or covered outside hallway

PRESERVE: to keep in good condition without change

PRESIDIO: a settlement of military men

QUADRANGLE: four-sided shape; the shape of most missions

RANCHOS:	large ranches often many miles from mission proper where crops were grown and animal herds grazed
REBUILD:	to build again; to repair a great deal of something
REPLICA:	a close copy of the original
REREDOS:	the wall behind the main altar inside the church
*RESTORATION:	to bring something back to its original condition (see * below)
SANCTUARY:	area inside, at the front of the church where the main altar is found
SECULARIZATION:	something not religious; a law in mission days taking the mission buildings away from the church and placing them under government rule
*ORIGINAL:	the first one; the first one built

BIBLIOGRAPHY

Bauer, Helen, *California Mission Days*. Sacramento, CA: California State Department of Education, 1957.

Bonestell, Chesler, and Johnson, Paul. *The Golden Era of the Missions, 1976-1834*. San Francisco, CA: Chronicle Books, 1974

Goodman, Marian. *Missions of California*. Redwood City Tribune, 1961

Sunset Editors. *The California Missions*. Menlo Park, CA: Lane Publishing Co., 1979.

Weber, Msgr. Francis J. ed. *The Penultimate Mission*. Hong Kong: Libra Press Limited, 1983

Wright, Ralph B., ed. *California Missions*. Arroyo Grande, CA 93420: Hubert A. Lowman, 1977.

For more information about this mission, write to:

Mission San Rafael
5th Ave. and A St.
San Rafael, CA 94901

It is best to enclose a self-addressed, stamped envelope and a small amount of money to pay for brochures and pictures the mission might send you.

Acknowledgement
Msgr. Thomas Kennedy

CREDITS

Cover art and Father Serra Illustration: Ellen Grim
Illustrations: Alfredo de Batuc
Ground Layout: Mary Boulé

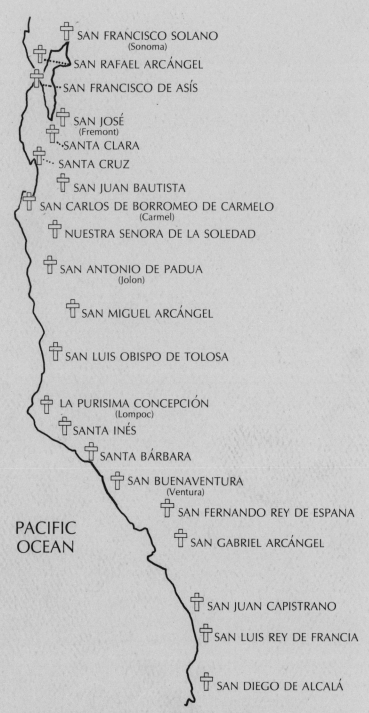

SAN FRANCISCO SOLANO
(Sonoma)

SAN RAFAEL ARCÁNGEL

SAN FRANCISCO DE ASÍS

SAN JOSÉ
(Fremont)

SANTA CLARA

SANTA CRUZ

SAN JUAN BAUTISTA

SAN CARLOS DE BORROMEO DE CARMELO
(Carmel)

NUESTRA SENORA DE LA SOLEDAD

SAN ANTONIO DE PADUA
(Jolon)

SAN MIGUEL ARCÁNGEL

SAN LUIS OBISPO DE TOLOSA

LA PURISIMA CONCEPCIÓN
(Lompoc)

SANTA INÉS

SANTA BÁRBARA

SAN BUENAVENTURA
(Ventura)

SAN FERNANDO REY DE ESPANA

SAN GABRIEL ARCÁNGEL

PACIFIC
OCEAN

SAN JUAN CAPISTRANO

SAN LUIS REY DE FRANCIA

SAN DIEGO DE ALCALÁ

NAME OF CITY IN PARENTHESES, IF OTHER THAN MISSION NAME

At last, a detailed book on the Mission San Rafael Arcángel written just for students

ABOUT THE AUTHOR

Mary Null Boulé has taught in the California Public School System for 25 years. Her past ten years as a fourth grade teacher made her aware of the necessity for a detailed informational book about the California missions. Five years of research, including visits to each mission, have resulted in this excellent series.

She is married and the mother of five grown children.

ISBN: 1-877599-19-0